A Biblical Worldview on
Heaven, Hell, and Eternity

HEAVEN

HELL

BIBLICAL
Worldview

Published in partnership between Andrew Wommack Ministries and Harrison House Publishers.

Woodland Park, CO 80863 – Shippensburg, PA 17257

ISBN 13 TP: 978-1-59548-645-5

ISBN 13 eBook: 978-1-6675-0952-5

For Worldwide Distribution.

1 2 3 4 5 6 / 27 26 25 24

CONTENTS

Note: This booklet is just a brief introduction to twelve hours of teaching from the Biblical Worldview: Heaven, Hell, and Eternity *curriculum. Statistics included in the* **"Did You Know?"** *and text sections of this booklet were cited when the complete curriculum was originally published and may no longer represent the most current information.*

Everyone views the world based on their beliefs—it's their worldview. As you process everything that you encounter, whether you know it or not, you are looking at it through a lens based on a variety of influences. You filter life based on experiences and factors from your background, such as where you grew up, family dynamics, ethnic heritage, religious upbringing, education and educators' views shared with students, and political views. Every day, your worldview guides your thoughts, decisions, and conversations.

It may surprise you to know that Christians don't automatically have a biblical worldview. When you became a Christian, you just began a journey to renew your mind. You did not automatically get a biblical worldview download at salvation. The problem many Christians face is a clash of worldviews. Often, it is difficult to recognize the daily assault on their Christian values and biblical teachings. Take note the next time you hear a news report or people sharing their perspectives and if you feel a twinge inside that indicates something isn't sitting right in your spirit. Typically, people are busy and ignore that twinge. When someone regularly encounters and hears perspectives that conflict with God's truth, that person can become dulled to it and simply begin to accept those perspectives as truth.

INTRODUCTION

Anyone who believes that the Bible is inspired by God (2 Tim. 3:16) must believe in life after death, or he must reject all that the Word of God says. Today, people are often swayed by someone else's experience of visiting heaven, returning from death, or encountering angels. These personal experiences should not be confused with what God's Word says about the afterlife. It is imperative to seek the truth, so you recognize falsehoods that lead to deception. This is not something you want to get wrong. Your eternal fate hinges on your choice in this life to accept or reject Jesus Christ.

Do you wonder about the afterlife and the End Times? Whether you believe in God or not, someday, you will die and face eternity. There are two vastly different destinations that are eternal—heaven and hell. The Word of God explains what these two destinations are like and what determines how people will spend eternity. When you learn what eternity with Jesus will be like, you will want to help others choose to make heaven their eternal choice.

This booklet will lead you on an expedition into what God inspired people to write about heaven, hell, and eternity. Many people are ignorant about life after death, whether through denial, misinformation, or very little information from the pulpits. God's Word has the answers to questions about the afterlife. When you know the truth, you can share the truth and impact someone's eternity!

CHAPTER 1

IS THERE LIFE AFTER DEATH?

by Andrew Wommack

Whether people want to talk about it or not, there is an afterlife. You can only go to one of two places—either heaven or hell. Some people base their reasoning about the afterlife on those who have died, come back, and tell their experiences, but that is subjective. You can't base your faith on what any person says about their experience. The Word of God is foundational, accurate, and trustworthy and shows that there is life after death.

Most people, even those who don't believe in an afterlife, will not be contentious over heaven because it's a place of blessing. But many Christians cannot believe that a loving God would send people to hell. We need to learn what God's Word says about hell.

Scripture makes it clear, and if you believe in the Bible, then you have to believe there is life after death (1 Thess. 4:13–18). If you don't believe that there is a resurrection, then the people who die are just gone. You'll never see them again. It's over. This belief increases grief. In 1 Thessalonians 4:14, Paul talks about how those who are asleep—those who've already died—are going to come back with the Lord. They do not stop existing. Those who have already died will be the first ones to have their body physically resurrected (1 Thess. 4:16). Believing in a resurrection and seeing our loved ones again is one of the ways that we comfort one another (1 Thess. 4:17–18). Without a physical resurrection, Christianity would be no different from all the other religions in the world.

Did You Know?

Christianity is the only religion where people make pilgrimages and travel to see an empty tomb. The founders of all the other major religions are dead and buried. You can find their remains. But Christians go to Jerusalem, look in the sepulcher, and see an empty tomb because Jesus was resurrected from the dead.

One reason that society is in the situation it's in today is the church has not been preaching about life after death, heaven and hell, and accountability. People don't fear judgment and being held accountable for their actions. Psalm 36:1 says, "*The transgression of the wicked saith within my heart* that there is *no fear of God before his eyes*." People are doing evil things, and ungodliness is running rampant. If you peel the layers back, they do not believe that there is a hell or a future judgment. They believe that when you die, that's it. Because of that, they commit mass shootings and then commit suicide and think that they escaped punishment. That's not so.

Today, people have been led to believe they are no different than animals, so they live like animals. This is why evolution is so popular, and people embrace it. They want to believe that they are not going to be held accountable for their actions, and that when they die, they just die. But that is not what the Word of God teaches. If people knew that they would have to give an accounting of their actions before God, we wouldn't have so much ungodliness running rampant.

Jesus taught there was life after death. This can clearly be seen when the Sadducees (who didn't believe in a resurrection) tried to trick him with a hypothetical story about a woman who was married to seven men who all died before her (Matt. 22:25-32). To answer them, Jesus cited the scripture from Exodus 3:6 where the Lord told Moses, I AM—not WAS—the God of Abraham, Isaac, and Jacob. These three patriarchs were still alive, even though they had died. That should settle the issue for anyone who believes in Jesus.

CHAPTER 2

ETERNITY: ONLY TWO OPTIONS

by Barry Bennett

When it comes to the topic of eternity, it is important that we have a personal understanding and revelation of what it is and what the options are. In John 3:16–17, we see the compassion and the heart of God—that He sent His only begotten Son. The caveat or the condition is that if we believe in Him, then we should not perish. God's heart is that men be saved. We see God's heart for humanity when Jesus became flesh and gave Himself for us. This provided the opportunity to know the truth (John 1:14), which means that the truth isn't obvious to everyone. There is a truth to be understood, received, and believed so that we do not perish. Every human on this earth is going to face one of two possible destinies that are going to last forever. Our time on this earth is very brief. We need to decide now where we are going to spend eternity.

Jesus talked about one of the options, heaven, in John 14:2, *"In My Father's house..."* where my Father dwells, *"are many mansions,"* or the more accurate word would be *abodes*,[1] or *dwelling places*. There are many places to reside. Jesus' intention and His heart is to go to this place where God lives and prepare a place for us with Him in heaven (John 14:3). Not only is He going to prepare a place for us, but He's also going to return again and receive us to Himself to be where He is. The Father wants us to be where He is because it's a place of fullness of joy where we will be His children and have everlasting life. Our finite, human minds can't conceive of the glories of heaven (1 Cor. 2:9–10). It's beyond human understanding, but the spirit can reveal these things to us.

Believers await transition into heaven with everlasting life, but what about other people? The unjust, who have not believed in the Lord, are choosing their eternity. They know there is a God, but they have hardened themselves to Him (Rom. 1:21). They know there is truth, but they suppress it, deny it, and do everything they can to get it out of their way. The unjust want to ignore the things of God so that they can indulge their flesh. The Bible states that the unjust will face punishment and judgment (2 Pet. 2:4 and 9).

Revelation 21:8 (NKJV) says, *"But the cowardly, unbelieving, abominable, murderers, sexually immoral, sorcerers, idolaters, and all liars shall have their part in the lake which burns with fire and brimstone, which is the second death."* This is the final judgment for those who hated the truth, hated the light, hated the love of the truth, loved the darkness, didn't want anything to do with God, and continued to live after the flesh. Their eternal destiny is the lake of fire. This is the second death.

Hell was never created for mankind. It was never the heart of God that men would suffer this destination. But men choose darkness, and they're going to get darkness for eternity. Jesus told the story of the rich man and Lazarus (Luke 16:19–31) to emphasize that hell and suffering are real. God is withholding the unjust under punishment, awaiting the day of judgment when they will be cast into the lake of fire forever. It will be everlasting, just as eternal life is everlasting.

Remember, it is not God's heart that anyone should perish. He desires all should come to repentance, to the knowledge of the truth, and to receive the love of the truth—Jesus. Jesus came to give us everlasting life. He came to give us a place in heaven and a relationship with the Father, where at His right hand are pleasures forevermore. While we are on this earth in this life, we have two options to choose from. The choice you make in this life to receive Jesus' salvation or reject Him settles your eternal destination—everlasting life with Jesus in heaven or eternal torment and separation from God in hell.

CHAPTER 3

WHAT IS HEAVEN LIKE?

by Rick McFarland

The Apostle Paul shows the stark contrast between this earth and heaven by pointing out that in heaven the old things pass away (2 Cor. 5:17). Christians experience a type of passing away at salvation. The old man or nature passed away, and all things became new in the new man or born-again spirit. Your physical body didn't change when you got saved, only your spirit changed. In heaven, all things will change, and everything dealing with your old body, your old experiences, and your old memories are going to change.

Another earthly thing that won't be in heaven is marriage among each other. On the earth, marriage is meant to last until physical death separates two people. According to Romans 7:2 (NKJV), "*For the woman who has a husband is bound by the law to her husband as long as he lives. But if the husband dies, she is released from the law of her husband.*" In heaven, marriage will not be between people but between Christ and the church (Eph. 5:31–32).

Did You Know?

There are three heavens. The first heaven is the space and the air around us—the earth's atmosphere—where we breathe air and pilots fly in the sky. The second heaven is outer space where the planets and stars are. Beyond, there's a third heaven called the place of God's dwelling and the paradise of God.

In heaven, you will receive a glorified body, like Jesus' glorified body (1 Cor. 15:49). When Jesus was in a glorified body, he could walk through walls (John 20:19) and travel from heaven in an instant. In our new bodies, we will dwell in heaven and come down to earth like angels. The angels dwell in the very presence of God, but they can manifest themselves on earth. Our glorified bodies will be able to come back with Jesus at the Second Coming, and we're going to rule and reign with Him on this earth for a thousand years (Rev. 20:6).

Here's a sampling of what the Bible tells us awaits us in heaven:

- Heaven will be a wonderful place of health, prosperity, peace, victory, and abundance. God's will is going to be fully manifested in heaven (Matt. 6:10).

- Heaven will be heavily populated. It's true that more people will reject Jesus and will go into everlasting punishment than those who actually choose Jesus. But over the ages, multitudes have accepted Jesus. (Rev. 7:9 and Heb. 12:22-23).

- Heaven will be a place of splendor and beauty. God is the God of prosperity, and this is reflected in the streets, walls, and gates of heaven (Rev. 21:18 and 21).

- Heaven is a place where we will eat food. Many people think we're just going to have spirits with no bodies. Yet, when Jesus' body was raised from the dead in a glorified resurrection body, He ate. The disciples gave Jesus a piece of broiled fish and some honeycomb, and He ate it (Luke 24:42–43). Also, Revelation 19:9 talks about the marriage supper.

- Heaven has perfect light all the time—no darkness or shadows. Where God dwells, there are no shadows. God is light, and heaven is going to be lit up everywhere without shadows.

Heaven will be filled with these wonders and more. But the greatest aspect of heaven will be the presence of Jesus. We will be with Him and see Him face to face. In heaven, we will dwell in the very presence of God, our Father, and our Savior, Jesus Christ (2 Cor. 5:8). The minute a believer dies, they're going to move into the very presence of their Savior and see Him face to face (Rev. 21:3 and 22:3-4).

CHAPTER 4

WHAT IS HELL LIKE?

by Mark Cowart

If you look at the turmoil and rampant ungodliness in the world and think you are currently living in hell, nothing could be further from the biblical truth. In Mark 9:42–48, the Lord made it clear that hell is going to be an absolutely horrible place of unquenchable fire and eternal suffering that affects three dimensions.

1. *There will be spiritual suffering.* To understand this aspect, you must recognize that you are a spirit, you have a soul, and you live in a body (1 Thess. 5:23). We were created in the image of God—in His likeness (Gen. 1:26–27). We are not God, but we're created in His image, so one of the things we know is that we can never die. This truth counters some people's worldview that souls in hell will eventually cease to exist because they will be

consumed and burned up. They incorrectly believe that a loving God would never punish anyone for an eternity. Our bodies die on this earth, but our spirits live forever. In heaven, your body will one day rejoin your spirit and never cease to exist. Hell will be a place that God withdraws Himself from because Satan and his cohorts will be there (Matt. 25:41). The spiritual element of hell will be the worst of all three elements.

2. *There will be soulish suffering*. Your soul is your mind, will, and emotions. Your soul and spirit make up what we call the human heart. Suffering registers in a person's soul. The soul will be fully intact in hell, and there will be memories and regret in hell.

3. *There will be bodily/physical suffering.* When people die, their bodies go into the earth, and then they go back to dust. If you're born again, you will receive a glorified body that won't age, won't have aches or pains, and will never know sickness or disease (1 Cor. 15:35–54). In heaven, there will be no more sorrow, no more tears, and no more crying

(Rev. 21:4). Hell is the direct contrast, where there will be continual weeping, torment, and gnashing of teeth (Luke 13:28 and 16:23–24).

Did You Know?

In ancient Jerusalem, there was a large garbage dump called Gehenna, which comes from the Hebrew name Valley of Hinnom. It is a type and shadow of the endless agonies of hell. Gehenna burned constantly with fire to consume the trash and carcasses, which would attract maggots and worms.[2]

Hell will be suffering in every dimension of life. Every part of a human being will be in torment and absolute excruciating pain. There will not be one part of a human being that will not be in absolute, undiluted, unrestricted hell: spiritually; soulishly of the mind, will, and the emotions; and physically. Think about what it would be like confined for all eternity in a place that the Bible describes as the lake of fire (Rev. 20:10 and 14-15). Then, recognize that hell is a place where we don't want anybody to go. There's not just a heaven to gain; there's a hell to shun. There is an urgency to share the Gospel with people so they will receive salvation, gain heaven, and avoid hell.

CHAPTER 5

HARD QUESTIONS ABOUT HEAVEN

by Alex McFarland

When looking for answers about the afterlife, it is imperative that God's Word and God's revelation be the definitive source of truth. Be aware, many people have accounts of supernatural experiences and have written books and become famous by talking about a message from an angel. In Galatians 1:8, the Word of God says that if even "*an angel from heaven*" preaches a different Gospel, "*let him be accursed*." Paul said that if we or even an angel says something contrary to God's revelation regarding salvation and the afterlife, we shouldn't listen to that. We do not want to be misled. Colossians 2:8 says to beware, lest anyone deceives you with vain, false philosophy. When it comes to issues of the afterlife, it is imperative that we stick to what God's Word says, and especially to what the Lord Jesus has said. Only

Jesus was able, under His own power, to go into the afterlife and come back alive to tell about it.

Will I see my child in heaven? Based on the Word of God, I believe the answer is yes. Babies go to heaven. Children go to heaven. The Lord Jesus said that if someone would harm a little child, it would be better to put a millstone around their neck and throw them in the depths of the sea (Luke 17:2). Jesus said to suffer the little children, forbid them not to come unto me "*for of such is the kingdom of heaven*" (Matt. 19:14). Prior to the age of accountability, children go to heaven because they're under God's grace. Jesus said the little children were of the kingdom of heaven. Children and those mentally incapable of making a salvation decision are of the kingdom of heaven because they're not morally accountable.

Will the mentally incompetent go to heaven? I believe they will because, while the person may have had the physical body of a forty-something, they had the mental capacity of an infant. Life is sacred in all contexts because we're made in the image of God. An infant who is alive but not fully mentally cognizant yet or a person with intellectual ability and volitional awareness held back will go to heaven. Why? Because God is a God of grace. The conscience of a child or a mentally incompetent person won't accuse them because they didn't reject something that they understood. A baby or mentally incompetent person can't stand before God and say, "Oh, I rejected Jesus," because they couldn't have known that.

What about the person born on the wrong continent who didn't hear about Jesus? All people will give an account to God (Rom. 14:12), and we are responsible for how we embraced the light that we had. Romans 2:14-16 talks about when the Gentiles, who didn't have the Law, by nature do the things prescribed in the Law. It shows that the Law is written on their hearts. There's a moral awareness in the hearts of all people.

It's been said that there is a heaven-sized hole in every human heart. Many people try to fill the hole with sex, drugs, or materialism. People long for justice, relationships restored, and wrongs made right—the way things will be in heaven. What the heart longs for is the Lord Jesus, and what we really desire is not any of the trinkets of this world but heaven. We're in the greatest love story and the greatest search and rescue mission of all time. God's Word promises that heaven is coming, and all will be made well.

The real question is not some hypothetical, "What about the person on the other side of the planet, or what about the mentally challenged?" The real question to be pondered is, "What have you done with Jesus?" Jesus asked, *"But who do you say that I am?"* (Luke 9:20 NKJV). Heaven is wonderful. Jesus wants you to be there, so make sure that you know Christ and invest your life to do your utmost to help others know Him as well.

CHAPTER 6

WHAT DOES ETERNITY SHOW US?

by Greg Mohr

You may feel like you've waited an "eternity" in a drive-thru line, or it takes "forever" for the food to warm in a microwave. When measuring time, perspective matters. A child may wait "an eternity" for their sixteenth birthday, yet as people age, time seems to fly by quickly. A person's lifespan is capped at 120 years according to Genesis 6:3 (NKJV), "*And the LORD said, 'My Spirit shall not strive with man forever, for he* is *indeed flesh; yet his days shall be one hundred and twenty years.'*"

When people breathe their last breath, eternity begins for them—there is no purgatory or second chances. Eternity is each person's final destination. The two eternal destinations, heaven or hell, come with vastly different judgments.

Although eternity is in the future, eternal life begins the moment a person receives Jesus Christ as Lord and Savior. At that moment of spiritual birth, the believer begins to prepare for their heavenly eternity where they will receive rewards and crowns at the judgment seat of Christ. That preparation includes choices to yield to the Lord, follow Him, and obey Him, but not obedience in a legalistic way. As you follow the Lord, yield yourself to Him, and live from your spirit man, you are preparing for an abundant entrance into the Kingdom of God.

At the judgment seat of Christ, each believer will stand before the Lord to receive their rewards based on what they did with what God called them to do in this life. God has a purpose and a plan for each person that includes touching other people, influencing other people for Jesus, and discipling other people. In fact, God created each person with a purpose before the world began (Rom. 11:29). He created you with a purpose to yield your life to Jesus, to accept Him as your Lord and Savior, so you can become a son or daughter of God. Then, you can use your unique gifts and calling as a platform to influence other people, touch other people, and manifest His love to other people.

Jesus will give crowns to Christians at the judgment seat of Christ. Second Timothy 4:7–8 (NKJV) says, "*I have fought the good fight, I have finished the race, I have kept the faith. Finally, there is laid up for me the crown of righteousness, which the Lord, the righteous Judge, will give to me on that Day, and not to me only but also to all who have loved His appearing.*" These crowns will be laid before the Lord's feet. The crowns will be awarded based on what you did in this life with your finances and your gifts. Your finances can be used now to affect eternity by sharing the Gospel to impact souls—that's the true riches. Your choices in this life have the potential to affect eternity. You can plunder hell and populate heaven based on how you live now. If you choose wisely to win souls, someday in heaven, people will stop by your mansion and say, "Thank you for yielding your life to Jesus."

What about the person who does not make the choice while on the earth to accept salvation through Jesus Christ? At the moment of death, that person will enter eternity apart from God.

The bottom line is that God will not force anyone to live with Him in eternity forever. The heaven or hell issue is determined by what you do with Jesus. Jesus is the only way to heaven according to John 14:6 (NKJV), "*Jesus said to him, 'I am the way, the truth, and the life. No one comes to the Father except through Me.'*" The choice is yours. Choose heaven!

CHAPTER 7

NEW HEAVEN, NEW EARTH, AND NEW JERUSALEM

by Greg Mohr and Rick McFarland

The timeline of future events found in the book of Revelation will begin with the Second Coming when Jesus returns to set up an earthly kingdom. After Jesus comes back, the judgment seat of Christ takes place, where the church will receive rewards for what it's done for the Lord. We're the bride of Christ, and there's going to be a great marriage supper. Revelation 19:9 (NKJV) says, "*Then he said to me, 'Write: "Blessed are those who are called to the marriage supper of the Lamb!"' And he said to me, 'These are the true sayings of God.'*"

Then, there will be a new heaven and a new earth (Rev. 21:1). In Revelation 21, we're going to see the heavens meet the earth. Heaven now is in the third heaven. The heavens are going to descend and actually rest over the new heaven and the new earth.

The light of heaven that will be coming down to rest over the earth will light up the earth. Revelation 21:1 conveys that the first earth and the first heaven pass away, and the oceans will be removed. Seventy percent of the current earth is water, which will increase living capacity. Revelation 21:2 reveals the New Jerusalem will come down and rest over the new earth. Revelation 21:4 points out there will be no more death or pain. But one day, He's going to wipe away those tears. There will be no pain, no memory of the hurt.

Revelation 21:9–10 mentions "the bride" and "the great city." The church is the bride of Christ, decked out in wonderful garments and jewels. We're actually going to inhabit the great city. Note the details given in scripture that acknowledge planning and grandeur, unlike anything on this earth.

- Revelation 21:12 and 14 says that the gates John saw had the names of the twelve tribes of the Old Testament. The twelve foundations had the apostles' names on them, implying that all the redeemed from the ages of the Old Testament and New Testament will inhabit this city. Verse 14 also points out there are twelve foundations, implying twelve levels to this city. This city is going to be colossal to accommodate the billions of people who have been saved throughout all time.

- Revelation 21:16 uses the measurement 12,000 furlongs, which is 1,500 miles.[3] So, each of the twelve levels of the New Jerusalem will be 1,500 miles long, 1,500 miles wide, and 1,500 miles high. Revelation 21:17 mentions the thickness of the wall, which today would equal about seventy-three yards thick.[4]

- Revelation 21:18 disproves the belief that God's not into wealth and prosperity because it says He will make His city and streets out of gold. The city will be made of the finest jewels without imperfection. God is an extravagant God. Revelation 21:23 talks about light, and on the Mount of Transfiguration, Jesus shone with great light (Matt 17:1–2). The light of Jesus will illuminate the entire city.

Then we enter the eternity of eternities. We're not just going to be passive inhabitants of heaven. We're going to be ruling and reigning forever. We're going to be judging angels, directing them, and telling them what to do. Heaven is not going to be a dull place. It's going to be a place of active participation and fulfillment of our purpose.

Our life has an end, even if it's 120 years. In light of eternity, James 4:14 says our life is a vapor in terms of its quantity. Heaven is coming down to earth. We're going to live forever, and it's for everyone whose name is written in the Lamb's Book of Life. These wonderful things about heaven aren't conjecture. These things are facts from God's Word, showing us our future. You don't have to be afraid of death if you know Jesus.

CHAPTER 8

THE SECOND COMING, RAPTURE, AND JUDGMENT DAY

by Andrew Wommack and Mark Cowart

Among Christians, there are differing interpretations of the scriptures regarding the Rapture, which is the end-times belief that both living and dead believers will ascend into heaven to meet Jesus Christ.[5] There is no need to be contentious about the Rapture. We all agree that the Lord is coming back, that we are going to be caught up with Him, and that the ungodly will stand judgment. The exact details of how it happens, when it happens, whether we get raptured out, or whether we go through some tribulations are open for debate.

Most Rapture theories fall under Pre-Tribulation: Christ will return before a seven-year period of intense tribulation to take His church (living and dead) into heaven;[6] or Post-Tribulation: There will be a Second Coming where Christ will return just before the millennium and just after a time of great apostasy and tribulation and believers will be caught up and changed in a moment, in the twinkling of an eye (1 Cor. 15:52).[7]

Those who agree with the Pre-Tribulation view believe the first three and a half years are going to be a time of pseudo-peace. They believe the body of Christ that is in the earth is what restrains the man of sin (the Antichrist). This belief is based on 2 Thessalonians 2:6–7, "*[6]And now ye know what withholdeth that he might be revealed in his time. [7]For the mystery of iniquity doth already work: only he who now letteth will let, until he be taken out of the way*." Not all Christians agree that the unnamed restraining force is the church.

Halfway through the Tribulation, the man of sin will be revealed, take off all the trappings, and it will be a time of persecution. Revelation 13 shows the Antichrist and the false prophet will wage war against anybody who doesn't worship them. They put up an image of the beast, and the false prophet commands it to come to life. Nobody knows exactly what this is going to be. It could be an animated image that looks like it's alive. The Antichrist will cause people to worship that image. Artificial intelligence and many things are leading up to this End Time. We're closer than ever to seeing how the man of sin, the Antichrist, could step in to take control. The stage is set for the Antichrist.

Andrew believes the reason people are motivated to believe in the Rapture is because the book of Revelation shows terrible persecution, and people don't want to experience any of the terrible things. You may believe God won't allow His people to endure terrible things, but it's already happening with about one hundred thousand Christians martyred every year right now.[8] During the ten plagues in the land of Egypt, the Israelites went through it, but while everybody else experienced the plagues, the Israelites didn't.

In eternity, what matters is whether you accepted salvation or not because the result will be one of the two judgments: the judgment seat of Christ and the Great White Throne of Judgment. The judgment seat of Christ is for believers, and rewards are given to them. The Great White Throne of Judgment is for unbelievers. It is the final, formal sentencing at the end of the millennial reign.

Revelation 20:14 says, *"And death and hell were cast into the lake of fire."* This is the consummation, the sealing, and the finishing of the dealings of God and man. And in that age-old contest where Lucifer, who became Satan, thought he would overthrow God, he loses.

We don't all have to agree on being pre- or post-Tribulation, but we can still love one another and love God. The most important thing in this life is that your name is written in the Lamb's Book of Life, and you received Jesus as your Savior and Lord.

CHAPTER 9

THE FATE OF THE UNBELIEVER
by Alex McFarland

Today, many preachers don't talk about hell because it is uncomfortable, but it is the somber reality that awaits unbelievers. Acts 20:27 (NKJV) reminds us of the duty "*to declare to you the whole counsel of God*." We don't cut, paste, pick, and choose things we will or won't discuss. If it's in the Bible, God put it there for a reason. The Bible is very clear about the promises of heaven, but it is equally clear about the realities and the warnings against hell.

Does the reality of eternal punishment contradict the love of God? No. We know it would not be righteous and just for Billy Graham to have the same fate as Osama bin Laden. Everybody has a sense of right and wrong. The Bible says that God punishes wickedness, and we should be glad that He does. He is a just God (Deut. 32:4). God doesn't judge from a human perspective (Rom. 2:5). God is a righteous judge (Ps. 119:137). Satan is at work in this world, but the day is coming when God will punish wickedness. For those who do not want Jesus, there is a place, and that place is called hell.

No one is in hell against their will. They didn't want to be there—but they didn't want to be in heaven in the presence of Christ either. Only God knows the human heart, how much enlightenment each person has been privy to, and to what degree we embraced or rejected known truth. The lost chose to be away from God.

To deny the reality of hell undermines the fixed nature of Christian revelation. God's revelation of sin, righteousness, and salvation is fixed, not fluid. It is eternal, not transient. And it is absolute, not subjective. We can't change God's revelation. Hell is necessary because God's righteous nature demands that sin be punished.

People often talk about their friend or relative who doesn't want anything to do with God but is a really good person. Don't fixate on your standard of deservedness, merit, or the assumed righteousness of someone, rather than the truth of the Savior who gave His life for us. Trusting Jesus Christ is what really matters.

> **Did You Know?**
>
> In colonial America, one of the most brilliant minds was one of the presidents of Princeton University, a man named Jonathan Edwards. He famously preached a sermon, "Sinners in the Hands of an Angry God." God used that sermon to ignite the Great Awakening. He said of hell that if even one sinner in world history was saved, then the mercy of God would've been eminently demonstrated. His point was that God does not *owe* anybody mercy or grace.[10]

The question is not, "How is God fair when some are lost?" The real question is, "Why should God shower so much mercy and patiently give opportunity after opportunity to hear the Gospel and get saved?" We can proclaim the warnings about hell, but we ought to have a tear in our eye when we do it. Our heart breaks for those who reject God by their choice and go to hell. Remember, that it is merciful and absolute grace that any person goes to heaven.

CHAPTER 10

A CALL TO ACTION: ETERNITY AWAITS

by Barry Bennett

When contemplating how you should choose to live now as you prepare for eternity, consider that this earth is like an airplane terminal or a train station. People arrive and leave all the time. We don't know how long we'll be here on the earth—ten minutes or a hundred years or longer. We don't know when our heart will stop beating, but we do know that it will happen. All of us, unless Jesus comes first, will step out of this body and into eternity.

Hebrews 9:27 (NKJV) says, "*And as it is appointed for men to die once, but after this the judgment.*" Are you ready for what's next? The thought of passing out of this body and into the next life scares people because they have not prepared their hearts (Ps. 112:8 and Heb. 13:9). Their heart is not established in everlasting life (Dan. 12:2 and John 3:36). Their heart is not established in the love of God (1 John 5:3). They begin to be fearful and don't know what they're going to do. Some people try to squeeze all they can out of this life because they don't know, or choose not to believe, there is an eternity.

Is this life more important to you than eternity, which does not end? Eternity with God offers you the opportunity to dwell in the family of God (John 1:12), the fullness of joy (Ps. 16:11), and peace that passes all understanding (Phil. 4:7). It offers you all these things forever. And yet some would prefer to waste their lives in this little brief blip of mortal life on a fallen earth. Don't let this temporary life be more important to you than your eternal destiny.

We all have possessions that are special to us and bring us joy, but it's a temporary joy. According to 2 Peter 3:10, it's all going to burn up. It's all temporary and will dissolve. Everything is going to be gone. None of our material possessions have any eternal value. When we think of things in that light, we realize we should invest in eternal things.

I want to live my life in a way that reflects the eternity that I will enjoy. I want to invest myself in my marriage in a way that shows the love of God. I don't want to be upset, angry, frustrated, or live selfishly. I want to be a giver for, "*It is more blessed to give than to receive*" (Acts 20:35). I want to be a giver of love, forgiveness, patience, and all of the fruit of the Spirit (Gal. 5:22–23). I want to be a godly influence for others so they can see there is an eternity that they have to choose.

Do you realize that your life impacts other people? How you walk, talk, treat your spouse, or treat your children impacts those around you. Those actions are seeds that you are sowing. People will see the love of God in you as your life reflects your eternal values. God's heart is that you have an abundant life now.

The degree to which you live an abundant life of peace, joy, and love influences the people around you. You can be a light in the darkness. God wants your life to be "*good … pressed down, shaken together, and running over*" (Luke 6:38 NKJV) and "t*o do exceedingly abundantly above all that we ask or think*" (Eph. 3:20 NKJV). That's the life that God wants you to live because He loves you and wants others to know Him through you. People will know how good God is when they see your blessed life. You can make choices now to intentionally impact others and influence them to consider their eternal destiny.

CONCLUSION

Many people think this life is all there is. They focus on having a good life now and living it to the fullest. When they face eternity someday, it will be too late to prepare for heaven. You've heard the truth, and you can't ignore the question: Will you choose heaven or hell? You can't change your mind after you die. You can make the most important decision of your life now to receive Jesus Christ as your Savior. This earth is temporal, but you can begin preparing now for eternity and your rewards in heaven.

The moment a person dies, they enter eternity. Imagine the joy of entering heaven someday and seeing people who are there because you shared the truth with them. Heaven will be full of worship and praising God throughout eternity. You will see Him face to face. In heaven, there are no tears, sickness, poverty, or death. God will be the light in heaven, and there will be no shadows. Make every moment now count for eternity. Boldly share the truth and introduce people to God's love and mercy that offers them the opportunity to spend eternity with Him.

CONTINUE BUILDING YOUR BIBLICAL WORLDVIEW

Every day, you are confronted with non-biblical worldviews coming to you through social media, the internet, and secular news sources. The Truth and Liberty Coalition (**truthandliberty.net**) can guide you to process current events through the lens of God's Word.

- *Truth and Liberty Show:* insight on current issues

- *Website:* resources include a 24/7 news feed, links to other online content related to biblical worldview and current American government issues, blogs, voter guides, and prayer guides

If you enjoyed this booklet and would like more tools to arm yourself with a biblical worldview, I suggest these teachings:

- *Biblical Worldview: Foundational Truths* (complete curriculum)
- *Eternal Life*
- *The Power of the Cross*
- *How to Deal with Grief*
- *The True Nature of God*
- *What Does the Bible Say About Hell?*

Some of these teachings are available for free at **awmi.net**, or they can be purchased at **awmi.net/store**.

RECEIVE JESUS AS YOUR SAVIOR

Choosing to receive Jesus Christ as your Lord and Savior is the most important decision you'll ever make!

God's Word promises, *"That if thou shalt confess with thy mouth the Lord Jesus, and shalt believe in thine heart that God hath raised him from the dead, thou shalt be saved. For with the heart man believeth unto righteousness; and with the mouth confession is made unto salvation"* (Rom. 10:9–10). *"For whosoever shall call upon the name of the Lord shall be saved"* (Rom. 10:13). By His grace, God has already done everything to provide salvation. Your part is simply to believe and receive.

Pray out loud: "Jesus, I confess that You are my Lord and Savior. I believe in my heart that God raised You from the dead. By faith in Your Word, I receive salvation now. Thank You for saving me."

The very moment you commit your life to Jesus

Christ, the truth of His Word instantly comes to pass in your spirit. Now that you're born again, there's a brand-new you!

Please contact us and let us know that you've prayed to receive Jesus as your Savior. We'd like to send you some free materials to help you on your new journey. Call our Helpline: **719-635-1111** (available 24 hours a day, seven days a week) to speak to a staff member who is here to help you understand and grow in your new relationship with the Lord.

Welcome to your new life!

RECEIVE THE HOLY SPIRIT

As His child, your loving heavenly Father wants to give you the supernatural power you need to live a new life. *"For every one that asketh receiveth; and he that seeketh findeth; and to him that knocketh it shall be opened...how much more shall your heavenly Father give the Holy Spirit to them that ask him?"* (Luke 11:10–13).

All you have to do is ask, believe, and receive!

Pray this: "Father, I recognize my need for Your power to live a new life. Please fill me with Your Holy Spirit. By faith, I receive it right now. Thank You for baptizing me. Holy Spirit, You are welcome in my life."

Some syllables from a language you don't recognize will rise up from your heart to your mouth (1 Cor. 14:14). As you speak them out loud by faith, you're releasing God's power from within and building yourself up in the spirit (1 Cor. 14:4). You can do this whenever and wherever you like.

It doesn't really matter whether you felt anything or not when you prayed to receive the Lord and His Spirit. If you believed in your heart that you received, then God's Word promises you did. *"Therefore I say unto you, What things soever ye desire, when ye pray, believe that ye receive* **them***, and ye shall have* **them***"* (Mark 11:24). God always honors His Word—believe it!

We would like to rejoice with you and help you understand more fully what has taken place in your life!

Please contact us to let us know that you've prayed to be filled with the Holy Spirit and to request the book *The New You & the Holy Spirit*. This book will explain in more detail about the benefits of being filled with the Holy Spirit and speaking in tongues. Call our Helpline: **719-635-1111** (available 24 hours a day, seven days a week).

CALL FOR PRAYER

If you need prayer for any reason, you can call our Helpline, 24 hours a day, seven days a week at **719-635-1111**. A trained prayer minister will answer your call and pray with you.

Every day, we receive testimonies of healings and other miracles from our Helpline, and we are ministering God's nearly-too-good-to-be-true message of the Gospel to more people than ever. So, I encourage you to call today!

ABOUT THE AUTHORS

Alex McFarland

Alex is a Christian apologist, author, evangelist, religion and culture analyst, and advocate for biblical truth. He speaks at Christian events, conferences, debates, and other venues to teach biblical truths and preach the Gospel. He has been a spokesperson on Fox News and other media outlets. Alex is the only evangelist to have preached in all fifty states in only fifty days. His "Tour of Truth" crusade swept across America with sixty-four evangelistic services from which came many decisions to receive Jesus and by which many Christians were equipped and encouraged. Find out more about Alex at **AlexMcFarland.com**.

Andrew Wommack

Andrew Wommack's life was forever changed the moment he encountered the supernatural love of God on March 23, 1968. As a renowned Bible teacher and author, Andrew has made it his mission to change the way the world sees God. Andrew's vision is to go as far and deep with the Gospel as possible. His message goes far through the *Gospel*

Truth television program, which is available to over half the world's population. The message goes deep through discipleship at Charis Bible College, headquartered in Woodland Park, Colorado. Founded in 1994, Charis has campuses across the United States and around the globe. Andrew also has an extensive library of teaching materials in print, audio, and video. More than 200,000 hours of free teachings can be accessed at **awmi.net**.

Barry Bennett

Barry Bennett is senior instructor at Charis Bible College. He is a graduate of Christ for the Nations Institute and served as a missionary in Mexico, Guatemala, and Chile for almost twelve years. Before becoming an instructor, Barry worked as a prayer minister in the phone center at Andrew Wommack Ministries and later took a position answering scriptural and doctrinal questions. Barry and his wife Betty Kay have three children and eight grandchildren.

Greg Mohr

Greg is a staff instructor at Charis Bible College, a conference speaker, and an author of several books. Previously, he served as senior pastor of River of Life Church in Decatur, Texas, for twenty-four years. Greg is a Rhema Bible Training Center graduate and has a master's degree in leadership from Southwestern Christian University. Greg serves as director of Ministry School at Charis and A.R.M.I. ministry ambassador. He and his wife Janice have four children and twelve grandchildren.

Mark Cowart

Mark and his wife Linda are senior pastors of Church For All Nations in Colorado Springs, Colorado. Mark serves as director of the Third-Year Practical Government School at Charis Bible College, as well as a member of the Truth & Liberty Coalition Board of Directors. He also co-hosts the Truth & Liberty live call-in show.

Rick McFarland

Rick is the senior pastor of River Rock Church in Colorado Springs. He graduated from both Oklahoma State University and Rhema Bible Training Center. He served Grace Church in Tulsa, Oklahoma, as the singles' pastor/director for twenty-six years then moved to Colorado in 2011 to attend Charis Bible College with his wife, Joann. In addition to pastoring, Rick serves as an adjunct instructor at Charis Bible College. Rick loves to study and is a lifelong student.

ENDNOTES

1. *Thayer's Greek-English Lexicon of the New Testament*, s.v. "μονή" ("monē"), accessed March 22, 2023, https://www.blueletterbible.org/lexicon/g3438/kjv/tr/0-1/.

2. Edwin Black, "Hell on Earth," *Washington Post*, August 29, 1999, https://www.washingtonpost.com/archive/lifestyle/1999/08/29/hell-on-earth/a2777d75-cfa6-4325-814a-0a26c83086c5; Easton's Bible Dictionary, s.v. "Gehenna," accessed April 24, 2023, https://www.blueletterbible.org/search/dictionary/viewtopic.cfm?topic=ET0001453.

3. "Convert Furlong to Mile," UnitConverters.net, accessed April 14, 2023, https://www.unitconverters.net/length/furlong-to-mile.htm.

4. "Convert Cubit (Greek) to Yard," UnitConverters.net, accessed July 24, 2024, https://www.unitconverters.net/length/cubit-greek-to-yard.htm.

5. *Encyclopedia Brittanica*, s.v. "Rapture," accessed June 26, 2023, https://www.britannica.com/topic/Rapture-the.

6. *Blue Letter Bible*, s.v. "Eschatology: Four Views on the Millennium," accessed July 3, 2023, https://www.blueletterbible.org/faq/mill.cfm.

7. *Blue Letter Bible*, s.v. "Eschatology: Four Views on the Millennium," accessed July 3, 2023, https://www.

blueletterbible.org/faq/mill.cfm.

8. Todd M. Johnson and Gina A. Zurlo, "Christian Martyrdom as a Pervasive Phenomenon (abstract and key findings)," *Global Society*, Volume 51, Issue 6 (December 2014): 679-685, https://link.springer.com/article/10.1007/s12115-014-9840-8.

9. This quote has been popularly attributed to William Booth. R.T. Kendall, *Unashamed to Bear His Name* (Grand Rapids, MI: Baker Publishing Group, 2012), 200, accessed March 20, 2023, https://archive.org/details/unashamedtobearh0000kend/page/n211/mode/2up.

10. J.C. Wolf, "*Jonathan Edwards on Evangelism*," Grand Rapids, Michigan: Wm. B. Eerdman's Publishing, 1958; pp. 25 and 126.

CONTACT INFORMATION

Andrew Wommack Ministries, Inc.

PO Box 3333

Colorado Springs, CO 80934-3333

info@awmi.net

awmi.net

Helpline: 719-635-1111 (available 24/7)

Charis Bible College

info@charisbiblecollege.org

844-360-9577

CharisBibleCollege.org

For a complete list of our offices, visit
awmi.net/contact-us.

Connect with us on social media.

www.ingramcontent.com/pod-product-compliance
Lightning Source LLC
Chambersburg PA
CBHW071638040426

42452CB00009B/1676